MIRACLES

CONNOR ALLEN
Illustrated by Amy Moody

LUCENT DREAMING

Second Edition

Miracles
Published by Lucent Dreaming Ltd.
103 Bute Street, Cardiff, CF10 5AD

First edition 2023. Reprinted 2024.

Copyright © 2024 Connor Allen and the children of Afon-Y-Felin and St. Andrew's Primary School.
All rights reserved. Printed in the United Kingdom by 4edge.
No part of this book may be reproduced without written permission from the author.

Connor Allen has asserted the author's right under the Copyright, Designs and Patents Act 1988 to be identified as author of this work.

Cover illustration by Amy Moody
Illustrations © 2024 Amy Moody

ISBN 978-1-916632-13-4

Lucent Dreaming acknowledges the financial support of Books Council of Wales and Creative Wales.

To every person that will pick up this book
This is for you

Always remember you're a miracle

CONTENTS

I

KNOCK KNOCK	8
BLANK CANVAS	10
THE HOPE	11
IN THESE TIMES	13
SOUTHWOOD ESTATE	14
TREDEGAR	15
POWIS CASTLE	16
THE KEYS TO THE FUTURE	17
KNOCK KNOCK: GRAN'S DOOR	18

II

I AM POEMS	21-39
SPECIAL MENTIONS	41-48

III

YOUR DOOR	51
ANYTHING YOU WANT TO BE	52
FIZZY	53
BLACK	54
WHAT IT MEANS TO BE A MUM	56
MOTHER/MUM	58
SUPERNOVA	59
THROUGH THE WINDOW	61
BOATS	62

SITTING ALONE	63
HOPE	64
SMILE	65
THE VALLEY	66
YOU	67
TRIBE	68
LOVE	69
FLYING	70
PATH THAT LIES AHEAD	71
MIRACLES	72

1

KNOCK KNOCK

I wonder
What's behind this door?
I hope it's not remnants of a time before.
Times that moved so fast,
And fragments of my past
That are rooted in pain,
Histories of shame
When I travel down memory lane.

But imagine
If behind this door
There's potential,
Not purpose,
As that's what's essential.

Because
Each and every one of us has magic
Contained within us.
To hope and dream of a better future is a must.

So, turn the handle,
Unlock the door,
Travel through,
And look upon
All those different variations of you.

There's
Strength,
Dreams,
Creativity
And so much more
And it's waiting for each and every one of you
Behind that door.

BLANK CANVAS

Life starts as a blank canvas.
With every stroke, every shade of the brush
You paint a picture.
A story is told
As your chapters unfold
In different poetic stanzas.
Your story,
Told how you like.
Your voice,
Echoing as it should.

Your mind is the most powerful tool.
Nobody can take that away from you.
The possibilities you envision,
The potential you're given,
That all comes from you.

Because

You're the future.
The next generation of leaders and healers,
Changemakers and inspirational speakers.
Just remember the future's bright
It's clear for all of Wales,
All of the world to see,
So ask yourself one question:
In this future
Who do I want to be?

THE HOPE

What does the future hold? No one really knows.
The effects of dominoes one by one falling.
Trees are planted. Across Wales they blossom.
The future generations are calling.

What will tomorrow bring? We can't always know.
Peace is what we're seeking.
Nature calls on us to explore her hidden beauties.
We are not voiceless. Listen when we're speaking.

What can today mould? The possibilities are endless.
The pressure is heavy but I know we can cope.
Grow tall, you trees. Grow tall to the sky.
All across Wales there are echoes of hope.

IN THESE TIMES

In these times of great uncertainty
2050 will have more plastic than fish in the sea
Humanity focused on deforestation, cutting down trees
We have to dream big and think smart

In these times of life below water and life on land
Let's protect the future, come take our hand
Plant blossoming trees from Snowdonia to Gower sands
Let's all make an impactful start

In these times where nature can be our friend
Exploring the hidden charm puts our souls on the mend
There's pockets of Welsh beauty I cannot comprehend
We need future generations to take part

In these times where connection to each other is essential
All across Wales, across generations, there's a sea of potential
Where if we come together the impact on the climate can be influential
There's hopefulness that fills my heart

SOUTHWOOD ESTATE

Walking through the fields
Cold wind blowing on my face
Insects, flowers, butterflies and bees
Can all find a home in this place

Sowing seeds to plant wildflowers
Cow poo fertilising the soil
Wildfires ravage, cause destruction
As the environment starts to boil

Wildflowers are important to attract insects
Wildflowers attract birds
Cows are free to roam
In the matriarchal herd

1822 a brick was laid
Southwood estate grew and grew
So much potential for wildlife
For the future beyond 2022

TREDEGAR

Handfuls of acorns
Chestnuts on the ground
Surrounded by fallen tree-trunks
It's peaceful, not a sound

Buildings have lived for centuries
Longer than you or me
Surviving through generations
Like the avenue of oak trees

Right to the top
Climbing the branches of the trees
The increased biodiversity is home
To brown-banded carder bees

Rainfall brings higher risks of flooding
For swans floating atop the boating lake
But within the nature of Tredegar
Breathe it in and take a break

POWIS CASTLE

A world-famous garden
On the doorstep of Wales
There's history rooted in the plants
And etched in red brick

Three hundred year old yew trees
Proudly standing guard
Apples and pears fill the garden
Free for all to pick

Like the sandwiches Paddington loves
The oranges make marmalade
Candy floss smells fill our nose
As we pass the midnight blues so quick

A penny in the fountain
So make a wish
Peacocks roam freely around
Regrowing their tails like magic

THE KEYS TO THE FUTURE

Is the world in a twilight zone?
Countless hours on mobile phones
Is that good or bad?
Does it make us happy or sad?
Some find comfort in games and TV,
Others find comfort in outdoor mysteries.

Sometimes we're lost,
Struggling with how to cope,
But we have to hold on to hope.
Whether that's through a screen,
Gaming with a group of friends,
Or outside in nature
Putting our souls on the mend.

The development of the world
It's mysterious to me,
Representing the future
The depths of our creativity.
It's limitless
Like our imaginations should be.

We hold the keys.

KNOCK KNOCK: GRAN'S DOOR

Knock knock
I wonder what's behind that door over there?
It's my gran
With her Jamaican accent, her Afro hair
It's her story
Connected to ancestors before
It's understanding
It's history
It's so much more

On the sandy shores
Of St Elizabeth
My gran
My family
My ancestors
Had a dream
With wind rushing through their hair
A few Jamaican pounds
The clothes that they wear

They brought with them
The music, culture
Language and food
Recipes for curried goat, jerk chicken
Packed as they travelled on the boats.
Gran brought with her the sand
From St Elizabeth beach
She brought stories, wisdom
Knowledge so she could teach
Her grandson
The rich history
The complexities
Between you and me.
The need to recognise
That we are strong
We are here and we belong
The understanding
Of where we are from

In 2022 like my ancestors before me
I have a dream
That hope and love
Will be the foundation
We use to travel upstream
To a better future where -
There's glory in difference
There's beauty in imperfection
Where we understand
BLACK has many shades
and many complexions.

II

During my tenure as Children's Laureate my whole aim and ethos was to empower children across Wales to consider themselves miracles. We are all unique, one in eight billion, and embracing individuality and uniqueness goes a long way to understanding that.

I had the absolute privilege of meeting and working with so many inspiring young people all over Wales over the past few years. As I aimed to empower them, and demystify poetry, I set them a task I borrowed from the wonderful Christina Thatcher in which they would write a simple list poem disguised in three columns, all about themselves and their likes.

The following section of the book showcases some of the amazing poems they have written, all of which highlight their individuality and uniqueness just that little bit more. All the poems in this section are from children aged between 9 and 11.

Layla

I am	Summer	because it is hot
I am	School	because we learn and get smart
I am	Flowers, Roses	because when I was a baby a rose fell on me
I am	Postman Pat	because the cat in Postman Pat
I am	Connor Allen and Family	because I love your poems

Seven

I am	Summer	my birthday
I am	Costa	love the drinks
I am	Candles	it's a beautiful smell
I am	Roblox	good games
I am	Family	because they do fun stuff with me and my sister

Holly

I am	Spring	because it's my birthday
I am	Pines Park	McDonald's
I am	Barbecue After	reminds me of where I was born
I am	My Bunny Stacy	it was because it was there since I was born
I am	Millie	she was my first best friend since I was one

Sophia

I am	Spring	all animals like lambs and calves are born
I am	Australia	because it has koalas and Bondi Beach
I am	Fairy Dust from Lush	delicious and reminds me of a baby smell
I am	My Doll Called Ellie	because my stepdad got it for me
I am	Mum	because my mum would do anything for me and she loves me no matter what

Evie

I am	Summer	bestie's birthday
I am	Paris	my uncle
I am	Candles	reminds me of my uncle because he died
I am	Jessie	it was the only toy I had =(
I am	My Bestie Lilla	Lilla was my bestie forever

Leo

I am	Autumn	birthday
I am	London	beautiful
I am	White Chocolate	hunger
I am	Dinosaur Teddy	nostalgia I've had it since I was one or two
I am	Gareth Bale	inspiration, Welsh legend

Sophie

I am	Summer	summer's my birthday
I am	Australia	my family lives there and you get to swim with sharks
I am	Pumpkin Pie Candle	reminds me of my nan
I am	Barbies/Bratz	it has loads of fashion
I am	Connor Allen	he inspires me to write poetry

Max

I am	Winter	I like playing with snow and my birthday
I am	Tenerife	I like Tenerife because the weather and the people are nice
I am	Snow Fairy	because it reminds me of joy
I am	Lego	I like Lego because I can get really creative with it
I am	Gabriel Jesus	I like Gabriel Jesus because he inspired me into playing football as my hobby

Lucy

I am	Summer	because I can tan and put my pool out
I am	Home	because when I am upset it's the best place to go
I am	Candles Vanilla	I like to smell vanilla because it reminds me of my sister
I am	My PS4	I like it because I can talk to my friends when I'm alone
I am	My Sister	when my uncle died my sister let me sleep over when I was upset and she inspires me to do good stuff

Rhylei

I am	Summer	because a pool to be cool
I am	My Nan's	because she feeds me steak
I am	Lavender	it's calming
I am	Toycar	it was my first toy car
I am	Everyone	because everyone is nice to me

James

I am	Summer	because I can take my pool out
I am	Principality Stadium	lets me think I will be there one day playing on that field
I am	McDonald's Muffin	because when my parents smell it they buy it
I am	PS5	it lets me talk to my friends
I am	Connor Allen	because he inspired me to love poetry and now I like poetry

Alfie

I am	Summer	because I get a tan
I am	My Home	I have a family
I am	My Mum's Perfume	it makes me feel happy and safe
I am	Drawing	it was given to me by my great nan I had it since I was one
I am	Everyone	because everyone is so nice and happy

Scott

I am	Winter	snowman
I am	Home	sleep
I am	McDonald's	food
I am	Car	cool
I am	Mum and Dad	Happy

Amelia

I am	Summer	because summer is my birthday
I am	My House	because it is with my family
I am	Connor's Clothes	because I love Connor and one day I'm going to be a poet
I am	Lego Friends	I like Lego because it keeps me calm
I am	My Mum	I love my mum because she is the world to me and she is ill

Charlie W.B

I am	Spring	Easter
I am	Paris	Disneyland Paris
I am	Rain	because it makes me feel relaxed
I am	Hot Wheels Supra	because I love cars
I am	My Nan	she got me my first Xbox and she gives me food

Bella

I am	Autumn	because of the colours
I am	London	because it's in my country and my memories
I am	Toffee	because it reminds me of when I was younger
I am	LOL Dolls	because my friends would come over and play with them with me when I was younger
I am	My Friends/Connie	because she comforts and makes other people happy and laugh and hug each other and caring for people

Owen

I am	Winter	winter is my favourite because I like playing in the snow
I am	Florida	because it has good weather
I am	Sea	the smell of the saltwater because it makes me thirsty
I am	Bop It	because it is fun to play with and it's cool
I am	Family	because they take care of me and make me happy

Charlie B

I am	Spring	bike riding
I am	France	camping
I am	Donuts	because it smells like flowers and cream
I am	Lego Technic	like building cars from it
I am	Dad	because he makes me laugh

Oliver

I am	Autumn	I love going outside
I am	Mexico	I love Spanish
I am	Kebab Meat	it reminds me that my family love me
I am	Stitch	I love Stitch because my sister gave it to me
I am	My Family	because my family help me

Ruby

I am	Summer	perfect time to spend with family
I am	Spain	because the food there
I am	McDonald's Chicken Nuggets	it's such a good smell and smells like yummy
I am	Monster High Dolls	because of the show and it's nostalgic
I am	My Family and Friends	they make me feel happy and inspired me and they comfort me and Lucy I have known her since 2016

TJM

I am	Summer	beach rugby
I am	Paris	RWC
I am	Pepperoni Pizza	the amazing taste
I am	Xbox	because I got something to do
I am	AJ	because he was my first friend since 2017

AJ

I am	Winter	because I like making snowmen
I am	Japan	because it has all my favourite anime
I am	Sea	makes me feel happy and hungry
I am	Teddy	because I had it for 5 years from my nan
I am	Nan	because my nan takes care of me and my brother and supports us in whatever we want and like to do and gives us food

Connie

I am	Spring	the weather is PERFECT
I am	Majorca	I have many memories there
I am	Vanilla	it's not too sweet it's just right
I am	My Cwtshies	they're nostalgic and I had them when I was born
I am	My Mam	because she's my mam and she loves me

George

I am	Summer	heat and warmth
I am	Nando's	spicy food
I am	A Warm Shower	reminds me of its comfort
I am	My Giant Among Us Teddy	my dad won it at Chessington the day after my ninth birthday in a giant claw machine
I am	Daisy or My Mum	because they're kind and nice

Emily J

I am	Summer	because it's sunny
I am	Home	it is warm
I am	Lavender	because it reminds me of trips
I am	Roblox	because it is exciting
I am	Connor	my favourite poet!

Bailey-Jai

I am	Summer	because it's hot
I am	My Bed	comfy
I am	Smelly Thing	just banging
I am	Football Try	fun to do tricks
I am	My Dad/Mum	they look after me and help me

Archie

I am	Summer	because I can go out places
I am	My Bed	because I can sleep
I am	Burger	because it's good
I am	Teddy called Tom	I had him when I broke my arm
I am	Jes and Rockey	because when I am sad they cwtch me

Enya

I am	Summer	it's hot! :) holiday
I am	:) My Bed	it's cozy
I am	Kinder Bueno Egg	it's delicious
I am	Slof Lollipop Teddy	he smells nice :) memories
I am	Lillie and Family	they're funny and my mum helps me a lot

Lillie

I am	Summer	it's hot and nice
I am	My Room	it's nice so I sleep in it
I am	Kinder	it smells like an Easter egg
I am	Minion/King Bob	he reminds me of Minions
I am	Family and Enya #1	she's funny and my family is cool and supportive

Demi

I am	Autumn	crunchy leaves
I am	McDonald's	because it's yummy
I am	Cheese and Chips	it smells so good
I am	My Teddies	because one of them belonged to my dead sister and they comfort me
I am	My Dog Amber	because she always there for me

Riley P

I am	Summer	you can go on a holiday
I am	Titanic	because it inspired me to draw
I am	Mum's Cooking	it has a lush smell to it
I am	Steve	he is one of the oldest plush I had and the first thing I had off Amazon
I am	Family	they keep me safe and they're always there for me

Oakley

I am	Summer	hot
I am	Home	family and somewhere to live
I am	Cake	makes me hungry
I am	iPhone	can call my friends and family when I need to
I am	Family and Polo My Cat	I love them and they make me happy

Gloria

I am	Summer	ice cream
I am	My Room	because I like drawing
I am	Chocolate	makes me want to eat more and more
I am	Bob the Unicorn	it gives me good memories
I am	Pet	helps me to learn how to take care of a pet

Liam

I am	Summer	because you can eat ice cream and u can sunbathe
I am	Disneyland	it's got rides magical and it's got the Marvel hotel
I am	Petrol	because it's got a strong smell
I am	iPhone	because it's got Emily's number
I am	Emily and Family	because they have everything that a person needs perfectly

Emily

I am	Summer	because it's holidays. Ice cream. Tan. Heat. My birthday.
I am	Disneyworld	because the rides, the characters and the heat
I am	My Nannie's Cooked Dinner	because the bread, chicken, gravy, peas, potato, yorkshires
I am	iPhones	because the games and Snapchat and I can text my friends and memory
I am	Family Best Friends Liam, Enya, Oakley	because I love them as family and friends

Lily

I am	Summer	because my birthday
I am	Spain	I get to explore
I am	Perfume - Lily Flower	because my name is Lily
I am	Squishmellow name is Sky	because I got it for my birthday
I am	Oliver My BFF	he makes me happy, joyful

Riley M

I am	Spring	because the flowers bloom
I am	Disneyland	because I can see the characters and vibe
I am	Burger	because it smells good and it's yummy
I am	Teddy	because I can punch it
I am	Miss Richards	because she is kind and teaches us. She is the best teacher in the world

Ffion

I am	Spring	my birthday
I am	Disneyland	it is fun and rides
I am	Fresh Baked Cakes	it smells super amazing and tastes good
I am	Doggy the Dog	it's the first toy I had and super soft
I am	Family and Friends	they are always there for me and if I am down they always make me up

Berjim

I am	Summer	I really like summer because I have 6 weeks off school and can smudge the ice cream on my face
I am	Turkey	where my family live
I am	Perfume	it makes me smell good
I am	Teddy Bear Mr Snuggles	it was my first teddy
I am	Mum/Dad	they support me

Shanaya

I am	Summer	6 weeks off, adventures
I am	Grandma's House	all of my family together
I am	Roast Dinner	it smells delicious and makes me want more
I am	Moo Moo	she was always there
I am	Fendi and Family	there when I need them at my low times and my best supporters

Theo

I am	Winter	snow
I am	Lanzarote	holiday
I am	Chilli Dogs	tasty
I am	Tails from Sonic the Hedgehog	he is funny
I am	My Family	amazing

Anthony

I am	Autumn	temperature
I am	House	fun
I am	Gasoline	gassy
I am	Ted the Teddybear	first toy given by someone special
I am	Mariøba Swierczska Mum and Micheal Dad	parents

Marcus

I am	Winter	so I can throw snowballs at my brother
I am	France	so I can learn French
I am	Corndog	because it smells nice
I am	Xbox	so I can play Minecraft and Roblox
I am	Michael Cox	so I can play with him and we help each other

Olivia P

I am	Summer	hot
I am	Disneyland	all of the rides
I am	Vanilla	it smells fresh
I am	iPhone	there is lots of games
I am	Family	they make me happy and laugh

Cole

I am	Summer	hot so you can play with friends
I am	Petrol Go-Karting	it's lots of fun with family
I am	Air Freshener	because it smells fresh
I am	Xbox	because you can talk to friends
I am	Family and Friends	makes you feel happy

Maddie

I am	Winter	stay cozy
I am	United States of America	lots of fun things
I am	Vanilla	makes me feel warm
I am	Phone	lots of apps
I am	Family	loved

Jorge

I am	Spring	it's my birthday and it's cute season
I am	Eiffel Tower	I love the view
I am	Fresh French Baguettes	they smell so good!
I am	My Big Jeff Teddy Bear	it was my first teddy
I am	My Mother and My Cat	my mum created me and my cat gives me comfort

Olivia L

I am	Winter	because there is snow
I am	Home	because of my bed
I am	Chocolate and Hot Chocolate	because it's delicious
I am	Bear ABC	because it's soft and I got it in a carnival
I am	Everyone	because they're special!!! All of them

Cohen

I am	Spring	hot months
I am	Spain	go on holiday and swim
I am	McDonald's Nuggets	they taste good
I am	Xbox	play games
I am	Cousin	we play together and I miss him

Light

I am	Summer	sunny holidays summer break and ice cream
I am	Burger King	their burgers taste delicious and I love going there with family
I am	Sir's Perfume	it was really strong and I love strong perfume
I am	Teddy (name is Teady)	because my mum bought it and I sleep with it every single day
I am	Whole Family Whole Friends Teachers	because they're all calm and cool to talk to

Gethin

I am	Autumn	it's my birthday
I am	Grandparents House	lots of fun + sweet memories
I am	Food	makes me excited to eat
I am	Plushie	I like to snuggle it at bedtime
I am	Mum + Dad	caring + comforting

Jace

I am	Summer	because we can go to the beach and I love the hot sun on my skin
I am	My Bed	it's my place to go when I am sad and angry
I am	Strawberries Candles	because it reminds me of my house and smells like my mum
I am	Basketball	because I love playing with it when I am sad and angry
I am	My Mum	because she is my everything my whole world and I would not be anything without her

SPECIAL MENTIONS

My mission as Children's Laureate was to empower children to use their voice by giving them the tools to tell their own stories. I met so many talented young people over the past few years whose writing and stories deeply moved me. These next three poems are special to me, each for their own reasons, and I wanted to highlight them in this book.

MY MAGICAL MEMORIES

Mum, Dad and I, went on holiday
Starting off in Dartmouth Bay
I sat by Mum on the boat ride
Excited to get to the other side

Went to Majorca on a plane
The journey was too wild for my brain
We sat by the pool waiting for the holiday club
Whilst Mum and Nan sat in the hot tub!

We started the day at the hotel
And pancakes were all that we could smell
Mum was dancing to Kou Kou move
She was really getting the groove

My mum loved to brush my hair
She loved to plait it with care
I loved the purple gem earrings she wore
Her purple, pretty necklaces hid away in the drawer

Her grey jumper was soft and cosy
She wore a dress, white and rosy
She loved to eat omelettes that she had made
My magical memories will never fade

Sophie, aged 9

WAR BROKEN SOULS

Dark cascading bombs,
Chipping away all of our life.
Together we're serving side by side,
Saving lives with burnt eyes.
Lips pry, as our "safe country"
Begins to fill with young and old cries.
Until you've ever completed your task,
And have thrown away your bombs.
You'd never known a loss,
Greater than we've faced or lost.
Half of our country, broken into,
Now there's no going back.
Creating forever craters in our homes,
We're in this war, fighting half alone.
Allies begin to come and go,
Saying bye to our "forever safe homes."

Now we're beginning to win this war,
Drenched in a mix of blood and gore.
Hoping that we still have a chance in life,
Souls have been broken, with a knife.
Please we ask, stop this war,
Please. Just stop, no more.
Now dead bodies fill our streets,
Hearts that once lived, have lost their beats.

Jaimeleigh, aged 16

I AM WALES!

I am the serrated, deadly talons, splitting through the rocky ground.

I am the inferno breath of fire, breathing over the calm, gentle clouds.

I am the petrifying, razor-sharp teeth, shredding the food away.

I am the gory, dripping jaws, ripping its prey apart.

I AM WALES!

I am the colossal, crumbling turrets, standing proudly to prevent its enemies.

I am the perishing, stony walls, smashing into smithereens on the precious floor.

I am the brave knight, stood to attention protecting the towering castle.

I am the powerful, sturdy drawbridge, carrying my people along to safety.

I AM WALES!

I am the supportive, cheerful fans, chanting the hard-working players on.

I am the clear, gleaming white try line, patiently waiting to be crossed.

I am the oval rugby ball, charging through the crystal blue sky.

I am the waving, uplifting flag, swaying from side to side to cheer Wales on.

I AM WALES!

I am the emerald green valley, positioned proudly while the shimmering yellow sun shines bright over the top of me.

I am the dazzling daffodils, growing joyfully underneath the crystal sky.

I am the overcoming mountain, stationed around the glistening river.

I am the woolly white sheep, grazing the vibrant green grass.

I AM WALES!

Skylah, aged 10

LAYERS OF MY SKIN

My skin is battered, my skin is beat,
Once innocent and soft, now dried to concrete.
I am suffocating in stereotypes and common ideologies,
Yet they expect my apologies.
When the police has no policy,
Is this what you call a democracy?
My life is built up these fears,
But I must hide behind my tears.

My skin is thick, my skin is tough,
Each dagger of bias makes me more rough.
Mockery and insults hit like whips and beams,
Yet my skin blocks out my sorrows screams.
I cry myself to sleep each night,
Keep my feelings bottled up out of sight.

My skin is scaled, my skin is burnt vast,
Time by time put in the furnace blast.
Scorch by the flames of humanity prejudice,
Showing courage and bravery means we are the nemesis.

Our ancestors fought valiantly so we could be here today,
Sacrificing all Rosa Parks, Mandela, MLK.
Yet they disgraced our heroes, our legacies blurred to lie,
Hundreds of years of oppression, forgotten in the blink of an eye.
But we took the tainted label and let them win,

We tried to change the colour of our skin.
Straightening the uniqueness from our hair,
Too Afraid to show our faces bare.

No matter how much we try to fit and we stood out,
But when we shouted for help, we were silenced throughout.
We tried to let the empty words keep us afloat,
Hours and hours of hard work, we would devote.
Yet the invisible chain of discrimination held us back,
Each day discrimination blows another attack.
So focused to fit in,
We sacrificed our culture, the true beauty of our skin.

My skin is scarred my skin is brutalised,
I don't deserve to be dehumanised.
Every nasty word insulting grin,
And every sky cut deeper than my skin.

My skin is judged my skin is conceptualised,
As everyone's hatred stares, I am paralysed.

I am judged by the colour of my skin,
No one dares to look within.

But I am tired of seeing lives shatter,
It is time to turn a new chapter.
My skin is beautiful, my skin is sweet,
We will not accept defeats.
Together, we will rise in this opportunity,

Create a safe space for all an inclusive community.
Layers of my skin, what makes me unique,
They have given me the courage to stand up and speak.
We may not all be from the same race,
But we can blossom together in the same place.
So anti-racist, we must be,
To move forward, we need to move in unity.

Anabia, aged 13

III

YOUR DOOR

There is no door in the entire universe
Exactly like your door
Unique in every single detail
Just for you to explore

Individual in its colours and patterns
From Barbie pink to TARDIS blue
Each door is different in so many ways
Harnessing the full potential of you

Behind your door is wonderful and new
Discoveries of every kind
Thousands of adventures and memories to make
And they all start in your mind
So
Open your door to magic
A world of treasures to view
A beautiful story yet to be uncovered
You'll find it if you walk on through

ANYTHING YOU WANT TO BE

You can be anything you want to be
Just set your imagination free
Set sail and your eyes will soon see
That you can be anything you want to be

You can go to university and get a degree
You can be a news reporter every evening on the BBC
You can travel the world from Asia to Jamaica to Tennessee
You can be an Oscar winner or even a Grammy nominee

You can be an NBA champion like JaVale McGee
You can be a footballer as great as Thierry Henry
You can be Stormzy on the pyramid stage at Glastonbury
You can be Colin Kaepernick and take a knee

You can be anything you want to be
Trust me and I guarantee
That with my words I'm giving you the key
To grow up and be anything you want to be

FIZZY

From the bubbles at the bottom
Building up and up
The absence
The lack of answers
Getting tough and tough.
This bottle
Houses so many gas bubbles:
Laughter, Anger,
Love, Sorrow,
Forgotten dreams and
Tears of a what could've been
Tomorrow.
The pressure builds
Feels like we're going to explode
Bubbles whizzing and colliding
Eruption of emotions
To decode.
Understanding these bubbles
Goes a long way
To figuring out how we're feeling
And if we're actually doing okay.

BLACK

When people look at me
Black isn't always what they see,
But Black is part of my ethnicity.
Black is in my family tree.
From Jamaica to Newport,
Black is a part of me.
Black is the features I got from my father.
Black is in the feelings that I harbour.
Black is the banter I share with my brother.
Black is in the music played by my mother.
Black is in the clothes I wear.
Black is the way I fix my hair.
Black is the heroes I aspire to be.
Black is in my genetic key.
Black is my cousins,
My aunty, my uncles, my nana.
Black is the way I talk,
It's in my grammar.
Black is in the people I look up to,
Like Stormzy, Viola, The Obamas.
Black is Tupac singing *Dear Mama*.
Black is the food I eat.
Black is Kobe winning a three-peat.
Black is in my history.
Black is the music I love on Kisstory.
Black is in my thoughts and fears.
Black is in my community of peers.

Black is in a lot of what I see,
But Black isn't all of me.
Black is in my bones.
It's in my glory.
But Black is only half of my story.
I'm so much more complex than black and white:
I'm a star, twinkling, shining so bright
With the power and potential to ignite
A spark to forge a future full of light.

WHAT IT MEANS TO BE A MUM

What it means to be a mum
Giving me Calpol when I've got a baddy tum
When I was a baby rubbing Sudocrem on my sore bum
Making delicious food that makes me go yum
Cheering me up when I'm feeling so glum

What it means to be a mum
Pushing me to race and chase my dreams
Making big bowls of strawberries and cream
Giving me advice because we're a team
Telling me straight when I'm being mean

What it means to be a mum
Wiping away my tears when I'm feeling sad
Calming me down when I'm so mad
Keeping the Action Men that I once had
Safe and sound it makes me so glad

What it means to be a mum
Driving me around from place to place
Singing along to music with such a deep bass
Teaching me how to tie my first shoelace
I left for uni you helped me pack my case

What it means to be a mum
Teaching me what it means to be a man
When no when else was there to say I can
Improvising at times when you had no plan
But always remember Mum I'm your number 1 fan

MOTHER
U
M

A mother is more than just one word or six letters.
They're that one person who makes everything better.
You can always rely on her 365 days of the year
Through all the uncertainty, laughter and tears.
Teaching how to change the gears on a bike
Or cooking a favourite meal, just what you like.
Holding your hand in a room that gives you a fright.
Giving you confidence when you discover something you dislike.
Even cleaning up your mess
When they themselves are super stressed
Coz there's no manual on being the perfect mum
But they juggle so much and get everything done.
No matter what they're always there
Giving love, dedication, time and care
When they themselves have had no rest,
And that's why mums are simply the best.

SUPERNOVA

When I was 11 I lost my best friend.
He became a star in the granite sky.
When I missed him Mum said look up
To the night and you'll see him fly.

Soaring through constellations and planets
He was up there shining bright,
Floating the depths of deep space
Through darkness, giving hope and light.

Leaping and meeting new civilisations,
He was touching the milky way,
Weaving in and out of Orion's belt,
A universe of games to play.

I look up and I know he's looking down.
My best friend he's watching over,
Perched in the ink of the night
Like the brightest supernova.

THROUGH THE WINDOW

Water fell from the sky in droplets of rain
I'm sat on my own in a carriage on a train
Staring out of the windowpane
At the souls that remain
Ones harbouring happiness
Some harbouring pain.

The window
Showing me everything that passes by
Reminiscing on times
When I was younger
Times I wished I could fly.

But you can't buy back time
That's not how it works
No matter how much deep down it hurts.
You have to stay hopeful
Of the future that's to come
Laid out in tiny little breadcrumbs
For us to succumb.

So let's learn to illuminate
What we're going through today
In a way that makes us stronger
And the storms of yesterday
Will linger no longer.

BOATS

Floating in a cold ocean
With different people
And a mixture of emotions.
All traveling in the same storm.
Yes, waves are getting choppy
But boats are never in the same form.
Not everyone is in the same boat:
Some in yachts, some in dinghies,
Some are strong, some are flimsy.
So whatever boat you're in
Just remember:
Keep hold of hope
And you'll stay afloat.

SITTING ALONE

Sitting alone
With thoughts and dreams
Catching them like fireflies
Putting them in different jars
Sitting alone
Smiling at the gleam
Upon a wooden shelf
Illuminating from afar
Sitting alone
Watching them float and beam
They will light the way
Beyond darkness
And straight to the stars

HOPE

Hope is the light to lead us
Out of darkness to better days
Paths paved with dreams
Empathy and compassionate ways
It infuses your future with ideas different and new
So much potential blossoms when Hope shines bright in you
Like a utopia
One where the future is brighter and better
Visions of Hope and vessels of Love
Echoing in our hearts forever

SMILE

I mean, what's in a smile?
You haven't smiled in a while
But that's OK
I can teach you
Coz I think it's overdue.
Look at all that potential in front of you
Or a beautiful place you like to view.
Think of someone who's always kind to you
Or even a day in the future you're looking forward to.

It's nice to smile,
Brings joy and positivity
That radiates for miles.
If someone's having a bad day
And they see a smile
It can change the way
They go about their day.
Smiles can come
In different shapes, sizes,
Colours and guises.
Huge or small.
Goofy or warm.
You can have one when you can barely crawl.
But most of all,
The one that shines above,
Is the smile on your face
That's full of love.

THE VALLEY

the bottom
of the valley
never has the clearest
view
so keep
on moving forward
to rise and start
anew

YOU

You are enough
YOU are always enough
And even when times are too tough
And the patches are so rough
Just remember
You. Are. Enough.

TRIBE

Search high and low, far and wide
For each and every member of your tribe
The ones who'll watch you ugly cry
The ones who'll help you grow and fly

Ones who are patient, ones who are kind
Ones who'll give you a moment of their time
Ones who'll cuddle you when the world isn't all it seems
Ones who'll push you to chase those dreams

Life is a marathon, not a sprint
So don't overthink
Take time to breathe and blink
And find those missing links

Friendships that last forever
They're something you can't describe
The ones who accept you for you
Are the best members of your tribe

LOVE

Love is the warmth of a cuddle
On days we find ourselves in a
Vacuum of self-doubt or struggle
Embracing our faith, family, friends or pets
In those times of deep sadness or utter regret
Shining like a diamond in the dark of the night
Holding your heart, cuddled ever so tight
Out of the darkness Love brings light
Paired with its cousin Hope it grows
Ensuring together the future stays bright

FLYING

I wish I could fly
straight up
to the pitch-black sky
And shine like a star
soaring across the universe
giving hope from afar

PATH THAT LIES AHEAD

Your future isn't written
On stone chapters of 'has to be'
It's written on magical pages
Of goals, ambitions and dreams

Your imagination is key
Be careful how you tread
Unlock your door to potential
To the path that lies ahead

Your future is yours
So dream big and be bold
You each hold the pen
To your story yet to be told

MIRACLES

The future you build lies before you,
Over waves of words you sail through.
It's a blueprint that's drawn in snow,
And every unique creation will show.

A sea of words floating upon your imagination,
You're a child on the waves of creation,
Climbing over mountains of make-belief,
Building a future, a sense of relief.

Words stored in the memory of the universe,
Like stars everlasting and diverse.
Light and treasure can be found in the dark,
And nothing can ever dim your spark.

One in eight billion, brilliant and unique,
Your potential is yours, and yours to seek.
Behind your door is magical and lyrical,
So walk on through as you are a miracle!

NOTES

p. 8 *Knock Knock* was commissioned by EYE Cymru in 2021.

p. 10 *Blank Canvas* was commissioned in March 2022 by Welsh Government to mark the historic event of physically punishing children becoming illegal in Wales.

p. 11 *The Hope* was commissioned by Literature Wales under Connor's laureateship.

p. 13 *In These Times* was commissioned by National Trust Cymru to launch their yearly #BlossomWatch campaign, and took inspiration from Maya Angelou's *In a time*.

p. 14-16 *Southwood Estate*, *Tredegar* and *Powis Castle* were all commissioned by National Trust Cymru to mark Youth Climate Action Day 2022 following a series of outdoor workshops on heritage sites with young people.

p. 17 *The Keys To The Future* was commissioned in 2022 by The Royal College of Psychiatrists in Wales.

p. 18 *Knock Knock: Gran's Door* was originally *Knock Knock 2*, commissioned by Literature Wales under Connor's laureateship to mark Black History Month 2022.

ACKNOWLEDGEMENTS

Christina,
Thank you for giving me the blueprint.
Eloise,
Thank you for laying the foundation.

Without those two phenomenal human beings there wouldn't be a Connor Allen Children's Laureate. I am blessed to have followed in the amazing footsteps of Eloise Williams who paved the path for me. And to Christina Thatcher who gave me the time and the tools to leave a lasting impact with my workshops and school visits. I have the utmost thanks and love for them both.

To Miriam I say thank you for your patience and understanding and for coming on this journey with me.

Mum and Blade I have to shout out because their constant belief in me allows me to fly to new heights and for that I love you both forever.

Dom - you'll never understand the impact you've had on me. My foundation of empowerment comes partly from our chats and the way you see the world. You keep me in check and for that you're part of my tribe.

Aunty Sharon - I'll never forget the message you bestowed upon me, "Connor, just be Connor."
You showed me we are all miracles.

Jannat and Lucent Dreaming thank you for your commitment and dedication to allow children everywhere to absorb themselves with these words and truly believe that they are miracles. This has been an incredible journey and you have played a monumental part in that.

And Amy, from the bottom of my heart, thank you for your talent and dedication in bringing your illustrations to these pages and helping create the world that is *Miracles*.

So many people have welcomed me over the duration of this laureateship, be it Jen at Swansea Libraries to Denise at Afon-Y-Felin. I have been allowed a truly unique gift of being able to inspire the next generation to believe in themselves and mould a future they can be proud of. The title *Miracles* didn't just happen overnight. It was a thought out idea from months and months of being allowed the honour to engage with truly unique individuals.

And to every child, parent, young person and adult who has believed in me and followed me during my time as Children's Laureate I have the biggest love and thanks for you because you have all given me the strength to carry on inspiring each and every day. You have all embraced my message of uniqueness and miracles and for that I am eternally grateful.

ABOUT THE AUTHOR

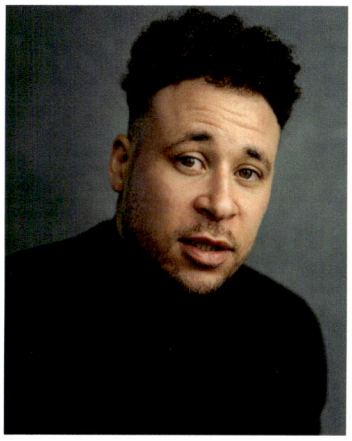

Connor Allen is an award-winning multidisciplinary artist and former Children's Laureate Wales (2021-2023). He has written for BBC Wales, BBC Radio 4, Wales Millennium Centre, Sherman Theatre, Dirty Protest, and others, and is a former member of the BBC Wales Welsh Voices and The Welsh Royal Court writing groups. His work is heavily inspired by elements of his own life including grief, love, masculinity, identity and ethnicity.

An actor graduate from Trinity Saint David, he wrote and performed in his acclaimed debut show *The Making of a Monster* at the Wales Millennium Centre in 2022 (playtext published by Aurora Metro Books). He was the 2023 winner of the Imison Award at the BBC Audio Drama Awards for his debut audio drama *The Making of a Monster*. In 2021, he won the Rising Star Wales Award, and was a Jerwood Live Work Fund recipient. *Dominoes*, his debut poetry collection for adults, was published in 2023. He is Associate Artist of his hometown theatre The Riverfront in Newport.